Best of
British
Cookbook

igloobooks

igloobooks

Published in 2015
by Igloo Books Ltd
Cottage Farm
Sywell
NN6 0BJ
www.igloobooks.com

Food photography and recipe development: PhotoCuisine UK
Front and back cover images © PhotoCuisine UK

HUN001 0615
2 4 6 8 10 9 7 5 3
ISBN 978-1-78343-447-3

Printed and manufactured in China

Contents

Starters

Potato and spring onion soup

PREPARATION TIME: 5 MINUTES I **COOKING TIME:** 30 MINUTES I **SERVES:** 4

INGREDIENTS:

12 spring onions (scallions)
2 tbsp olive oil
2 tbsp butter
2 cloves of garlic, crushed
3 medium potatoes, cubed
1 litre / 1 pint 15 fl. oz / 4 cups vegetable stock
salt and black pepper

PREPARATION METHOD

1. Slice the spring onions, reserving the green tops for a garnish.

2. Heat the oil and butter in a saucepan and fry the spring onions for 5 minutes or until softened.

3. Add the garlic and potatoes to the pan and cook for 2 more minutes, then stir in the vegetable stock and heat until it reaches boiling point.

4. Simmer for 20 minutes or until the potatoes are very tender, then blend until smooth with an emersion blender.

5. Season to taste with salt and pepper, then ladle into bowls and garnish with the reserved spring onion tops.

Egg and bacon muffins

PREPARATION TIME: 5 MINUTES I **COOKING TIME:** 5 MINUTES I **SERVES:** 2

INGREDIENTS:

2 English breakfast muffins, halved horizontally
1 tbsp butter
4 rashers streaky bacon
1 tbsp sunflower oil
2 large eggs

PREPARATION METHOD

1. Toast the muffin halves and spread them with butter.

2. Cook the bacon under a hot grill until crisp.

3. While the bacon is cooking, heat the oil in a non-stick frying pan and fry the eggs until the whites are set but the yolks are still a little runny.

4. Fill the muffins with the bacon and eggs and serve immediately.

Full English breakfast

PREPARATION TIME: 45 MINUTES I **COOKING TIME:** 35 MINUTES I **SERVES:** 4

INGREDIENTS:

2 tbsp sunflower oil
4 pork sausages
8 thick slices black pudding
8 rashers smoked streaky bacon
2 tomatoes, halved
400 g / 14 oz / 1 ¾ cups canned baked beans
white toast to serve

For the hash browns:
450 g / 1 lb waxy potatoes
½ onion, thinly sliced
1 tsp English mustard
1 large egg white
2 tbsp butter
salt and black pepper

PREPARATION METHOD

1. To make the hash browns, cook the unpeeled potatoes in boiling water for 18 minutes or until a skewer slides in easily. Drain well, then leave to cool completely before peeling.

2. Coarsely grate the potatoes, then stir in the onion. Whisk the mustard into the egg white and season with salt and pepper, then stir it into the potatoes. Shape the mixture into eight flat patties then chill for 30 minutes.

3. Melt the butter in a large frying pan then fry the hash browns over a low heat for 15 minutes, turning halfway through. Keep warm in a low oven.

4. Add the oil to the frying pan and fry the sausages for 10 minutes, turning regularly. Add the black pudding to the pan and cook for a further 5 minutes, turning everything half way through.

5. While the sausages are cooking, grill the bacon and tomatoes until the bacon is crisp and the tomatoes are hot in the centre. Bring the beans to a gentle simmer in a small saucepan.

6. Divide everything between four warm plates and season with salt and pepper. Serve immediately with white toast on the side.

Watercress soup with crispy bacon

PREPARATION TIME: 10 MINUTES I **COOKING TIME:** 10 MINUTES I **SERVES:** 4

INGREDIENTS:

2 tbsp olive oil
2 tbsp butter
1 small onion, chopped
2 cloves of garlic, crushed
1 litre / 1 pint 15 fl. oz / 4 cups
   vegetable stock

200 g / 7 oz / 6 cups watercress, washed
8 thin rashers smoked streaky bacon,
   halved
salt and black pepper

PREPARATION METHOD

1. Heat the oil and butter in a saucepan and
    fry the onion and garlic for 5 minutes or
    until softened, but not coloured.

2. Pour in the vegetable stock and heat until
    it reaches boiling point, then stir in the
    watercress. As soon as the stock comes
    back to the boil, ladle the soup into a
    liquidiser and blend until smooth. Season
    to taste with salt and pepper.

3. Cook the bacon under a very hot grill until
    very crisp.

4. Ladle the soup into four warm bowls and
    garnish with the crispy bacon.

Breadless Scotch eggs

PREPARATION TIME: 15 MINUTES I **COOKING TIME:** 25 MINUTES I **MAKES:** 6

INGREDIENTS:

6 small eggs
6 good quality pork sausages
6 rashers streaky bacon

PREPARATION METHOD

1. Preheat the oven to 180°C (160°C fan) / 350F / gas 4.

2. Put the eggs in a pan of cold water then bring to a simmer and cook for 5 minutes. Plunge the eggs into cold water for 2 minutes then peel off the shells.

3. Skin the sausages and divide the meat into 6. Flatten a portion of sausage meat onto your hand and put an egg in the centre, then squeeze the meat round the outside to coat. Repeat with the other 5 eggs.

4. Wrap each egg in bacon then transfer to a roasting tin. Roast the Scotch eggs for 20 minutes or until the sausage meat is cooked through. Serve hot or cold.

Caramelised onion sausage rolls

PREPARATION TIME: 35 MINUTES | **COOKING TIME:** 45 MINUTES | **MAKES:** 6

INGREDIENTS:

3 tbsp olive oil
2 onions, sliced
500 g / 1 lb 2 oz / 2½ cups all-butter puff
  pastry
350 g / 12 oz / 2 cups sausagemeat
1 egg, beaten
salt and black pepper

PREPARATION METHOD

1. Heat the oil in a large frying pan then fry the onions over a low heat for 20 minutes, stirring occasionally. Season with salt and pepper to taste, then leave to cool completely.

2. Preheat the oven to 220°C (200°C fan) / 425F / gas 7.

3. Roll out the pastry on a lightly floured surface into a large rectangle and cut in half lengthways. Top with the fried onions, then shape the sausagemeat into 2 long sausages the length of the pastry strips and lay them on top.

4. Fold over the pastry to enclose and seal the edge with beaten egg, pressing down firmly to seal. Cut each roll into 3 lengths and transfer them to a baking tray.

5. Brush the tops with beaten egg and lightly score the tops, then bake for 25 minutes or until golden brown and cooked through.

Pork pies

PREPARATION TIME: 1 HOUR | **COOKING TIME:** 45 MINUTES | **COOLING TIME:** 4 HOURS
MAKES: 4

INGREDIENTS:

200 g / 7 oz / 1 ⅓ cups minced pork
200 g / 7 oz / 1 ⅓ cups pork loin, finely
  chopped
100 g / 3 ½ oz / ⅔ cup back bacon, finely
  chopped
1 onion, finely grated
½ tsp ground white pepper
¼ tsp ground mace
175 ml / 6 fl. oz / ⅔ cup chicken stock
2 sheets leaf gelatine

For the pastry:
50 g / 1 ¾ oz / ¼ cup butter
200 g / 7 oz / 1 ⅓ cups plain (all-purpose)
  flour
50 g / 1 ¾ cups / ⅓ cup strong white
  bread flour
50 g / 1 ¾ oz / ¼ cup lard
1 large egg, beaten
salt and black pepper

PREPARATION METHOD

1. First make the pastry. Rub the butter into the two flours with 1 tsp of salt until the mixture resembles fine breadcrumbs. Put the lard in a saucepan with 100 ml water and heat until it reached boiling point, then stir it into the flour.

2. Turn the dough out onto a lightly floured work surface and knead for 1 minute or until smooth. Reserve a quarter of the dough for making the lids then divide the rest into four and shape using a pork pie dolly.

3. Mix the mince, pork loin, bacon, onion, and spices together, seasoning liberally with sea salt. Pack the mixture into the pastry cases.

4. Roll out the reserved pastry and cut out four lids. Brush around the rim of the pies with beaten egg, lay the lids on top, and crimp round the edges. Make a couple of

holes in the top of each pie for the steam to escape.

5. Chill for 30 minutes to firm up the pastry.

6. Preheat the oven to 200˚C (180˚C fan) / 400F / gas 6. Brush the pies with beaten egg and bake for 45 minutes.

7. Soak the gelatine in cold water for 10 minutes. Put the chicken stock in a small saucepan and bring to a simmer, then take it off the heat and whisk in the gelatine. When the pies are ready, remove them from the oven and leave to cool on a wire rack for 15 minutes. Insert the nozzle of a funnel into the steam holes and top up each pie with chicken stock. Leave the pies to cool and set for at least 4 hours or overnight before serving.

Tomato and thyme soup

PREPARATION TIME: 5 MINUTES | **COOKING TIME:** 30 MINUTES | **SERVES:** 4

INGREDIENTS:

2 tbsp olive oil
1 onion, finely chopped
4 cloves of garlic, crushed
2 tbsp thyme leaves
450 g / 1 lb ripe / 3 cups tomatoes, diced
500 ml / 17 ½ fl. oz / 2 cups vegetable stock
salt and black pepper

PREPARATION METHOD

1. Heat the oil in a saucepan and fry the onion for 8 minutes or until softened.

2. Add the garlic and half of the thyme to the pan and cook for 2 more minutes, then stir in the tomatoes and vegetable stock and heat until it reaches boiling point.

3. Simmer for 20 minutes then blend until smooth with a liquidiser or stick blender.

4. Taste the soup and adjust the seasoning with salt and pepper, then ladle into bowls and sprinkle with the rest of the thyme.

Classic Dinners

Beef wellington

PREPARATION TIME: 1 HOUR I **COOKING TIME:** 35 MINUTES I **SERVES:** 8

INGREDIENTS:

750 g / 1 lb 7 oz piece beef fillet
4 tbsp olive oil
2 tbsp butter
1 large onion, finely chopped
3 cloves of garlic, crushed
2 tbsp fresh thyme leaves

300 g / 10 ½ oz / 2 cups mushrooms, finely
  chopped
450 g / 1 lb / 2 cups all-butter puff pastry
1 egg, beaten
salt and black pepper

PREPARATION METHOD

1. Trim the beef of any sinew, then season well with sea salt and black pepper. Heat half of the oil in a large frying pan until smoking hot, then sear the beef on all sides until nicely coloured. Leave to cool.

2. Add the rest of the oil and the butter to the pan and turn the heat down to medium. Fry the onion for 5 minutes until it looks translucent, then add the garlic and thyme and cook for another minute, stirring all the time. Add the mushrooms and a pinch of salt and cook for 10 minutes or until the liquid that comes out has completely evaporated. Season to taste with salt and pepper, then leave to cool. Blend to a smooth puree in a food processor.

3. Preheat the oven to 230°C (210°C fan) / 450F / gas 8. Roll out the pastry on a floured surface into a large rectangle. Spread over the mushroom mixture, then sit the beef on top and enclose in the pastry. Crimp the edges and trim away any excess pastry, then brush with beaten egg. Decorate the top with the pastry trimmings, attaching with beaten egg.

4. Bake for 35 minutes or until the pastry is golden and cooked through underneath.

Cottage pie

PREPARATION TIME: 1 HOUR 20 MINUTES I **COOKING TIME:** 1 HOUR 30 MINUTES
SERVES: 4

INGREDIENTS:

2 tbsp olive oil
1 small onion, finely chopped
2 cloves of garlic, crushed
450 g / 1 lb / 2 cups minced beef
400 g / 14 oz / 1 ¾ cups canned tomatoes,
    chopped
400 ml / 14 fl. oz / 1 ⅔ cups beef stock

For the topping:
450 g / 1 lb / 2 ½ cups floury potatoes,
    peeled and cubed
100 ml / 3 ½ fl. oz / ½ cup milk
50 g / 1 ¾ oz / ¼ cup butter
50 g / 1 ¾ oz / ½ cup Cheddar, grated
salt and black pepper

PREPARATION METHOD

1. Heat the oil in a large saucepan and fry the
    onion for 3 minutes, stirring occasionally.
    Add the garlic and cook for 2 minutes, then
    add the mince. Fry the mince until it starts
    to brown then add the chopped tomatoes
    and stock and bring to a gentle simmer.

2. Cook for 1 hour, stirring occasionally,
    until the mince is tender and the sauce has
    thickened a little. Taste for seasoning and
    add salt and freshly ground black pepper
    as necessary.

3. Meanwhile, cook the potatoes in salted
    water for 10 minutes, or until they are
    tender, then drain well. Return the potatoes
    to the saucepan and add the milk and
    butter. Mash the potatoes until smooth.

4. Preheat the oven to 200°C (180°C fan) /
    400F / gas 6.

5. Spoon the mince mixture into a large
    baking dish then top with the mashed
    potatoes. Sprinkle over the grated cheese
    and bake in the oven for 20 minutes or
    until golden brown.

Lamb hotpot

PREPARATION TIME: 30 MINUTES I **COOKING TIME:** 1 HOURS 40 MINUTES I **SERVES:** 6

INGREDIENTS:

900 g / 2 lb / 6 cups boneless lamb
   neck, cubed
2 lamb kidneys, trimmed and quartered
50 g / 1 ¾ oz / ¼ cup butter
2 tbsp olive oil
2 onions, sliced
a few sprigs of thyme

1 tbsp plain (all-purpose) flour
800 ml / 1 pint 8 oz / 3 ¼ cups lamb stock
900 g / 2 lb / 4 cups potatoes, cut into thin
   slices
salt and black pepper

PREPARATION METHOD

1. Preheat the oven to 160°C (140°C fan) /
    325F / gas 3 and season the lamb liberally
    with salt and pepper.

2. Melt half the butter with the oil in a frying
    pan over a high heat then sear the lamb
    and kidneys in batches until browned
    all over. Remove the meat from the pan,
    lower the heat and add the onions. Cook
    for 5 minutes, stirring occasionally until
    softened. Add the garlic and thyme and
    cook for 2 more minutes.

3. Increase the heat and stir in the flour
    then incorporate the stock and bring to
    a simmer. Arrange the lamb and kidneys
    in a casserole dish and pour over the
    onion liquer.

4. Arrange the potatoes on top of the lamb,
    then cut the remaining butter into small
    pieces and dot it over the top of the
    potatoes. Cover the dish tightly with foil
    or a lid.

5. Bake the hotpot for 1 hour 30 minutes then
    remove the lid and cook for a further hour.

Roast lamb loin with chilli and garlic

PREPARATION TIME: 20 MINUTES I **COOKING TIME:** 25 MINUTES I **SERVES:** 4

INGREDIENTS:

5 large mild green chillies (chilies)
9 cloves of garlic
150 g / 5 ½ oz / ¾ cup soft goats' cheese
500 g / 1 lb 2 oz lamb loin, boned and rolled
salt and black pepper

PREPARATION METHOD

1. Preheat the oven to 220°C (200°C fan) / 425F / gas 7.

2. Finely chop one of the chillies and one of the garlic cloves, then mix them with the goats' cheese and season with salt and pepper.

3. Un-roll the lamb and spread it with the goats' cheese mixture, then roll it back up and re-tie it.

4. Transfer the lamb to a roasting tin with the rest of the chillies and garlic. Drizzle everything with oil and season with salt and pepper.

5. Transfer the tin to the oven and immediately reduce the temperature to 190°C (170°C fan) / 375F / gas 5.

6. Roast the lamb for 25 minutes or until cooked to your liking. Transfer the lamb to a warm serving plate, then cover with foil and leave to rest for 10 minutes before serving.

Steak and mushroom pie

PREPARATION TIME: 2 HOURS 30 MINUTES I **COOKING TIME:** 30 MINUTES I **SERVES:** 4

INGREDIENTS:

4 tbsp olive oil
1 kg / 2 lb 3 oz / 7 cups braising
   steak, cubed
1 onion, finely chopped
3 cloves of garlic, finely chopped
2 bay leaves

600 ml / 1 pint / 2 ½ cups good quality
   beef stock
250 g / 9 oz / 3 cups mushrooms, quartered
225 g / 8 oz / 1 cup all-butter puff pastry
1 egg, beaten

PREPARATION METHOD

1. Heat the oil in an oven-proof saucepan and sear the steak in batches until well browned. Remove the meat from the pan, add the onions, garlic, and bay leaves and cook for 5 minutes.

2. Pour in the stock and return the beef, then simmer for 2 hours. 30 minutes before the end of the cooking time, season to taste with salt and pepper and stir in the mushrooms. Leave to cool completely.

3. Preheat the oven to 220°C (200°C fan) / 425F / gas 7.

4. Ladle the pie filling into a baking dish and brush round the edge with beaten egg.

5. Roll out the pastry and lay it over the top of the pie, then trim away any excess. Press firmly round the outside to seal, then brush with beaten egg and make a hole for the steam to escape.

6. Bake the pie for 30 minutes or until the pastry is golden brown and cooked through.

Pot-roasted duck legs

PREPARATION TIME: 15 MINUTES I **COOKING TIME:** 1 HOUR 5 MINS I **SERVES:** 2

INGREDIENTS:

2 tbsp olive oil
2 duck leg quarters
2 shallots, finely chopped
1 clove of garlic, finely chopped
200 ml / 7 fl. oz / ¾ cup red wine
2 fresh figs, halved
salt and black pepper

PREPARATION METHOD

1. Preheat the oven to 180°C (160°C fan) / 350F / gas 4.

2. Heat the oil in a cast iron casserole dish. Season the duck well with salt and pepper, then sear on all sides until nicely browned.

3. Remove the duck from the pan then gently fry the shallots and garlic for 5 minutes. Stir in the wine, then bring to the boil. Return the duck legs to the pan, then cover and cook in the oven for 45 minutes.

4. Add the figs to the pot and return to the oven for a further 15 minutes with the lid off.

Rabbit stewed with broad beans

PREPARATION TIME: 1 MINUTES I **COOKING TIME:** 1 HOUR 30 MINUTES I **SERVES:** 4

INGREDIENTS:

4 rabbit saddles, each cut across into
   3 cutlets
3 tbsp plain (all-purpose) flour
1 tsp mustard powder
3 tbsp olive oil
2 tbsp butter
1 onion, finely chopped

2 cloves of garlic, finely chopped
a few sprigs of rosemary
150 ml / 5 ½ fl. oz / ⅔ cups Marsala
350 ml / 12 ½ fl. oz / 1 ½ cups chicken stock
300 g / 10 ½ oz / 2 cups broad (fava) beans,
   podded weight
salt and black pepper

PREPARATION METHOD

1. Season the rabbit well with salt and pepper,
    then toss with the flour and mustard
    powder to coat.

2. Heat half of the oil and butter in a casserole
    dish or saucepan and sear the rabbit pieces
    on all sides.

3. Remove the rabbit from the pan and add
    the rest of the oil and butter, followed by
    the onions, garlic, and rosemary.

4. Sauté for 5 minutes, then pour in the wine
    and stock and bring to a simmer. Transfer
    the rabbit back to the pan, then simmer
    very gently for 1 hour.

5. Stir in the beans, season to taste with
    salt and pepper and cook for a further
    15 minutes or until the rabbit is tender.

Sausagemeat pie

PREPARATION TIME: 1 HOUR | **COOKING TIME:** 20 MINUTES | **SERVES:** 4

INGREDIENTS:

2 tbsp olive oil
1 small onion, finely chopped
2 cloves of garlic, crushed
450 g / 1 lb / 2 cups pork sausagemeat
400 ml / 14 fl. oz / 1 ⅔ cups beef stock

For the topping:

450 g / 1 lb / 2 ½ cups floury potatoes,
   peeled and cubed
100 ml / 3 ½ fl. oz / ½ cup milk
50 g / 1 ¾ oz / ¼ cup butter
flat leaf parsley to garnish

PREPARATION METHOD

1. Heat the oil in a large saucepan and fry the onion for 3 minutes, stirring occasionally. Add the garlic and cook for 2 minutes, then add the sausagemeat, breaking it up with the spoon. Fry the sausagemeat until it starts to brown then add the stock and bring to a gentle simmer.

2. Cook for 30 minutes, stirring occasionally, until the meat is tender and the sauce has thickened a little. Taste for seasoning and add salt and freshly ground black pepper as necessary.

3. Meanwhile, cook the potatoes in salted water for 10 minutes, or until they are tender, then drain well. Return the potatoes to the saucepan and add the milk and butter. Mash the potatoes until smooth.

4. Preheat the oven to 200°C (180°C fan) / 400F / gas 6.

5. Spoon the sausagemeat mixture into a large baking dish then top with the mashed potatoes. Level the top then bake in the oven for 20 minutes or until golden brown. Garnish with parsley.

Ox cheek and carrot stew

PREPARATION TIME: 10 MINUTES I **COOKING TIME:** 3 HOURS I **SERVES:** 4

INGREDIENTS:

3 tbsp olive oil
800 g / 1 lb 12 oz ox cheek
1 onion, chopped
3 carrots, sliced
2 bay leaves
1 tbsp tomato puree

350 ml / 12 ½ fl. oz / 1 ½ cups stout
300 ml / 10 ½ fl. oz / 1 ¼ cups beef stock
salt and black pepper

PREPARATION METHOD

1. Heat the oil in a saucepan then season the ox cheek with salt and pepper and brown it well all over.

2. Remove the ox cheek from the pan and add the onion and carrots. Sauté for 5 minutes, then stir in the bay leaves and tomato puree.

3. Pour in the stout and stock and bring to a gentle simmer, then return the ox cheek to the pan, put on a lid, and stew very gently for 3 hours.

4. Taste the sauce for seasoning and add salt and pepper as necessary before serving.

Individual sausage cauliflower cheese

PREPARATION TIME: 20 MINUTES | **COOKING TIME:** 35 MINUTES | **MAKES:** 4

INGREDIENTS:

400 g / 14 oz cauliflower, cubed
2 tbsp olive oil
8 chipolata sausages
2 tbsp butter
2 tbsp plain (all-purpose) flour
600 ml / 1 pint / 2 ½ cups milk

150 g / 5 ½ oz Cheddar, grated
freshly grated nutmeg for sprinkling
salt and black pepper

PREPARATION METHOD

1. Preheat the oven to 180°C (160°C fan) / 350F / gas 4.

2. Cook the cauliflower in boiling, salted water for 6 minutes or until almost cooked, then drain well.

3. Meanwhile, heat the oil in a frying pan and brown the sausages all over.

4. Melt the butter in a medium saucepan then stir in the flour. Gradually whisk in the milk a little at a time until it is all incorporated. Cook the sauce over a low heat, stirring constantly, until the mixture thickens. Beat vigorously to remove any lumps.

5. Take the pan off the heat and stir in the cauliflower and half of the cheese. Season to taste with salt and pepper. Divide the mixture between four gratin dishes, press two sausages into the top of each one and sprinkle with the remaining cheese.

6. Sprinkle with nutmeg and bake for 25 minutes or until the tops are golden brown and the sausages are cooked.

Smoked haddock with mash

PREPARATION TIME: 30 MINUTES I **COOKING TIME:** 30 MINUTES I **SERVES:** 4

INGREDIENTS:

450 g / 1 lb / 2 ½ floury potatoes, peeled and cubed
500 ml / 17 ½ fl. oz / 2 cups milk
1 bay leaf
400 g / 14 oz un-dyed smoked haddock fillet
4 tbsp butter
2 tbsp plain (all-purpose) flour

1 tbsp flat leaf parsley, finely chopped
1 tbsp chives, finely chopped
1 tbsp basil leaves, finely chopped, plus extra to garnish
150 g / 5 ½ oz / 1 cup cherry tomatoes, quartered
salt and black pepper

PREPARATION METHOD

1. Cook the potatoes in boiling salted water for 12 minutes or until tender then drain well.

2. Meanwhile, put the milk and bay leaf in a small saucepan and bring to a simmer. Lay the haddock in a snugly-fitting dish and pour the hot milk over the top. Cover the dish with cling film and leave to stand for 10 minutes.

3. Heat half of the butter in a small saucepan and stir in the flour. Reserve 2 tbsp of the haddock milk for the potatoes and strain the rest into the butter and flour mixture, stirring constantly. Cook until the sauce is thick and smooth, then stir in the herbs and season with salt and pepper.

4. Mash the potatoes with the reserved milk and remaining butter and divide it between four warm bowls. Remove any skin and bones from the haddock then break it into large chunks and arrange on top.

5. Spoon over the sauce and serve with the cherry tomatoes on the side.

Beef and herb cobbler

PREPARATION TIME: 15 MINUTES I **COOKING TIME:** 3 HOURS 20 MINUTES I **SERVES:** 6

INGREDIENTS:

2 tbsp plain (all-purpose) flour
1 tsp mustard powder
900 g / 2 lb / 6 cups braising steak, cubed
4 tbsp olive oil
1 onion, finely chopped
3 cloves of garlic, finely chopped
4 sprigs thyme
2 bay leaves
600 ml / 1 pint / 2 ½ cups stout
600 ml / 1 pint / 2 ½ cups good quality
  beef stock
salt and black pepper

For the cobbles:

75 g / 2 ½ oz / ⅓ cup butter, cubed
250 g / 9 oz / 1 ⅔ cups self-raising flour,
  plus extra for dusting
½ tsp mustard powder
¼ tsp cayenne pepper
150 ml / 5 ½ fl. oz / ⅔ cup milk, plus extra
  for brushing
100 g / 3 ½ oz / 1 cup Red Leicester cheese,
  grated
2 tbsp flat leaf parsley, finely chopped
1 tbsp tarragon, finely chopped
1 tbsp chives, finely chopped
salt and black pepper

PREPARATION METHOD

1. Preheat the oven to 140°C (120°C fan) /
   275F / gas 1.

2. Mix the flour with the mustard powder and
   a good pinch of salt and pepper and toss it
   with the beef to coat. Heat half of the oil in
   a large cast iron casserole dish then sear
   the meat in batches until well browned.

3. Remove the beef from the pan, add the
   rest of the oil and cook the onions, garlic,
   and herbs for 5 minutes. Pour in the stout
   and boil for 5 minutes then add the stock
   to the pan and return the beef. Bring the
   casserole to a gentle simmer then put on
   a lid, transfer it to the oven, and cook for
   2 hours 30 minutes.

4. To make the cobbles, rub the butter into the
   flour with your fingertips until the mixture
   resembles fine breadcrumbs then stir in the
   mustard powder and cayenne pepper. Add
   the milk, cheese, and herbs mix together
   into a pliable dough.

5. Turn the dough out onto a floured work
   surface and flatten it into a rectangle, 2 cm
   (1 in) thick, then cut it into squares.

6. Arrange the cobbles on top of the casserole
   and return to the oven. Turn up the
   temperature to 200°C (180°C fan) / 400F /
   gas 6 and bake for 30 minutes.

Lamb and fresh apricot stew

PREPARATION TIME: 5 MINUTES I **COOK TIME:** 1 HOUR 30 MINUTES I **SERVES:** 6

INGREDIENTS:

800 g / 1 lb 12 oz / 5 ⅓ cups lamb shoulder, cubed
2 tsp ras el hanout spice mix
2 tbsp olive oil
2 tbsp honey
4 spring onions (scallions), sliced
3 cloves of garlic, finely chopped

50 g / 1 ¾ oz / ¼ cup sultanas
500 ml / 17 ½ fl. oz / 2 cups good quality lamb stock
12 fresh apricots, halved and stoned
75 g / 2 ½ oz / ½ cup blanched almonds
sea salt

PREPARATION METHOD

1. Preheat the oven to 160°C (140°C fan) / 325F / gas 3.

2. Put the lamb, spices, oil, honey, onions, garlic, and sultanas in a large tagine with a big pinch of salt and stir well to mix.

3. Pour over the stock then put on the lid and transfer the tagine to the oven.

4. Cook the tagine for 1 hour 15 minutes, then stir in the apricots and almonds and return to the oven for 15 minutes.

Roasts

Roast pork loin with sage

PREPARATION TIME: 15 MINUTES I **COOKING TIME:** 55 MINUTES I **SERVES:** 4

INGREDIENTS:

4-bone pork loin, trimmed
150 ml / 5 ½ fl. oz / ⅔ cup dry white wine
a handful of sage leaves
salt and black pepper

PREPARATION METHOD

1. Preheat the oven to 230°C (210°C fan) /
   450F / gas 8.

2. Sit the pork in a roasting tin and pour over
   the wine. Season with salt and pepper and
   scatter the sage leaves over and around.

3. Roast the pork for 10 minutes, then reduce
   the temperature to 180°C (160°C fan) / 350F
   / gas 4 and roast for a further 45 minutes,
   basting halfway through.

4. Cover the pan with a double layer of foil
   and leave the pork to rest for 10 minutes
   before carving into chops.

Roast beef stuffed with cheese

PREPARATION TIME: 15 MINUTES | **COOKING TIME:** 45 MINUTES | **SERVES:** 8

INGREDIENTS:

2 tbsp olive oil
1 kg / 2 lb 3 oz topside of beef
200 g / 7 oz / 1 ½ cups Cheddar, sliced
4 tbsp pesto
100 g / 3 ½ oz / ½ cup sun-blush
   tomatoes, chopped
salt and black pepper

PREPARATION METHOD

1. Preheat the oven to 200°C (180°C fan) / 400F / gas 6.

2. Heat the oil in a large oven-proof frying pan. Season the beef well with salt and pepper then sear it on all sides.

3. Slice the beef almost in half horizontally and stuff with the cheese, pesto and tomatoes. Secure closed with 2 skewers, then transfer to a baking dish and roast for 45 minutes.

4. Cover the beef with a double layer of foil and leave to rest in a warm place for 10 minutes before carving into thick slices.

Roast lamb with garlic and rosemary

PREPARATION TIME: 2 HOURS I **COOKING TIME:** 1 HOUR 10 MINUTES I **SERVES:** 6

INGREDIENTS:

3 cloves of garlic, crushed
1 tbsp rosemary leaves, finely chopped
3 tbsp olive oil
1.5 kg / 3 lb 5 ½ oz boned, rolled lamb leg
salt and black pepper

PREPARATION METHOD

1. Mix the garlic, rosemary, and oil into a paste and season with salt and pepper. Rub the mixture over the lamb and leave to marinate for 2 hours or overnight.

2. Preheat the oven to 220°C (200°C fan) / 425F / gas 7.

3. Roast the lamb for 25 minutes, then turn the oven down to 190°C (170°C fan) / 375F / gas 5 and roast for a further 45 minutes.

4. Transfer the lamb to a warm plate and cover with a double layer of foil and a towel. Leave to rest for 15 minutes before carving.

Roast chicken

PREPARATION TIME: 10 MINUTES | **COOKING TIME:** 1 HOUR 10 MINUTES | **SERVES:** 4

INGREDIENTS:

1.5 kg / 3 lb 5 oz chicken
3 tbsp olive oil
1 lemon, halved
1 bulb of garlic, halved horizontally
a few sprigs of thyme, plus extra to garnish
salt and black pepper

PREPARATION METHOD

1. Preheat the oven to 200°C (180°C fan) /
    400F / gas 6.

2. Season the chicken all over with sea salt
    and black pepper, then drizzle with olive
    oil and lay it breast side down in a large
    roasting tin. Put half of the lemon and
    garlic and all of the thyme inside the body
    cavity, and lay the rest of the lemon and
    garlic next to the chicken in the tin.

3. Transfer the tin to the oven and roast for
    30 minutes.

4. Turn the chicken breast side up and baste it
    with any juices from the tin, then roast for
    a further 40 minutes.

5. To test if the chicken is cooked, insert a
    skewer into the thickest part of the thigh.
    If the juices run clear with no trace of
    blood, it is ready.

6. Squeeze over the lemon halves and garnish
    with fresh thyme before serving.

Roast beef with onions and thyme

PREPARATION TIME: 15 MINUTES I **COOKING TIME:** 45 MINUTES I **SERVES:** 8

INGREDIENTS:

2 tbsp beef dripping
1 kg / 2 lb 3 oz topside of beef
2 red onions, sliced
2 white onions, sliced
a few sprigs of thyme
salt and black pepper

PREPARATION METHOD

1. Preheat the oven to 200°C (180°C fan) / 400F / gas 6.

2. Heat the dripping in a large oven-proof frying pan. Season the beef well with salt and pepper then sear it on all sides.

3. Transfer the beef to a baking dish and surround it with the onions, then roast for 45 minutes, stirring the onions every 15 minutes.

4. Cover the beef with a double layer of foil and leave to rest in a warm place for 10 minutes before carving.

Mustard-roasted collar bacon

PREPARATION TIME: 25 MINUTES I **COOKING TIME:** 2 HOURS 25 MINUTES I **SERVES:** 8

INGREDIENTS:

3 kg / 6 lb 8 oz whole collar bacon
2 carrots, in large chunks
2 celery sticks, in large chunks
2 onions, in large chunks
1 tbsp black peppercorns
2 bay leaves
3 tbsp Dijon mustard

3 tbsp grain mustard
4 cloves of garlic, unpeeled
a small bunch of thyme

PREPARATION METHOD

1. Put the collar bacon in a saucepan of cold water. Heat to boiling then discard the water.

2. Add the vegetables to the pan with enough cold water to cover the meat by 5 cm (2 in). Bring to a gentle simmer and skim any scum off the surface. Add the peppercorns and bay leaves, then put on a lid and simmer gently for 2 hours.

3. Remove the bacon from the saucepan and leave to steam dry in a baking dish for 5 minutes.

4. Preheat the oven to 220°C (200°C fan) / 425F / gas 7.

5. Mix the 2 mustards together and slather it over the collar bacon. Add the garlic cloves to the dish and sprinkle over the thyme.

6. Transfer the bacon to the oven and roast for 20 minutes. Serve hot or leave to cool completely before slicing and serving cold.

Stuffed turkey breast

PREPARATION TIME: 20 MINUTES I **COOKING TIME:** 40 MINUTES I **SERVES:** 6

INGREDIENTS:

250 g / 9 oz / 1 ¼ cups cooked chestnuts
1 large egg
30 g / 1 oz / ⅓ cup fresh white breadcrumbs
50 ml / 1 ¾ oz / ¼ cup milk
2 shallots, finely chopped
900 g / 2 lb turkey breast

50 g / 1 ¾ oz / ¼ cup butter, softened
salt and black pepper

PREPARATION METHOD

1. Reserve five chestnuts and put the rest in a food processor with the egg, breadcrumbs, milk and shallots. Blend to a fine puree.

2. Roughly chop the reserved chestnuts and stir them into the stuffing, then season well with salt and pepper.

3. Cut the turkey breast almost in half horizontally without cutting all the way through, then open it out like a book. Spoon the stuffing in a line down the centre, then fold the turkey back over and tie securely with string.

4. Preheat the oven to 220°C (200°C fan) / 425F / gas 7.

5. Lay the turkey in a greaseproof paper-lined roasting tin and smear with butter. Season with salt and pepper, then roast for 40 minutes or until the turkey is cooked all the way through. Carve into slices to serve.

Pub Grub

Sausage casserole

PREPARATION TIME: 15 MINUTES I **COOKING TIME:** 1 HOUR I **SERVES:** 4

INGREDIENTS:

2 tbsp olive oil
450 g / 1 lb sausages
1 onion, sliced
2 carrots, chopped
a few sprigs of thyme
1 litre / 1 pint 15 fl. oz / 4 cups
vegetable stock

PREPARATION METHOD

1. Heat the oil in a large cast iron casserole dish and brown the sausages all over. Remove from the pan and add the onion, carrots, and thyme and fry for 5 minutes.

2. Add the stock and heat to boiling.

3. Turn down the heat and simmer with the lid on for 1 hour. Season to taste before serving.

Steak and kidney pot pies

PREPARATION TIME: 30 MINUTES | **COOKING TIME:** 2 HOURS 35 MINUTES | **MAKES:** 6

INGREDIENTS:

4 tbsp olive oil
900 g / 2 lb / 6 cups braising steak, cubed
4 lamb's kidneys, trimmed and cubed
1 onion, finely chopped
3 cloves of garlic, finely chopped
2 bay leaves

600 ml / 1 pint / 2 ½ cups good quality
   beef stock
250 g / 9 oz / 3 cups mushrooms, quartered
225 g / 8 oz / 1 cup all-butter puff pastry
1 egg, beaten
salt and black pepper

PREPARATION METHOD

1. Heat the oil in an oven-proof saucepan and sear the steak and kidney in batches until well browned. Remove the meat from the pan, add the onions, garlic, and bay leaves and cook for 5 minutes.

2. Pour in the stock and return the beef, then simmer for 2 hours.

3. 30 minutes before the end of the cooking time, season to taste with salt and pepper and stir in the mushrooms. Leave to cool completely, then divide the filling between 6 individual pie dishes.

4. Preheat the oven to 220°C (200°C fan) / 425F / gas 7.

5. Roll out the pastry and cut out 6 circles a little larger in diameter than the top of the pie dishes. Lay the pastry on top of the filling and brush with beaten egg.

6. Bake the pies for 30 minutes or until the pastry is golden brown and cooked through.

Fish and vegetable potato-topped pie

PREPARATION TIME: 30 MINUTES I **COOKING TIME:** 55 MINUTES I **SERVES:** 4

INGREDIENTS:

450 g / 1 lb floury potatoes, peeled
    and cubed
500 ml / 17 ½ fl. oz / 2 cups milk
1 bay leaf
400 g / 14 oz smoked haddock fillet
4 tbsp butter

2 tbsp plain (all-purpose) flour
1 carrot, coarsely grated
1 courgette (zucchini), coarsely grated
1 yellow pepper, very thinly sliced
75 g / 2 ½ oz / ¾ cup Cheddar, grated
salt and black pepper

PREPARATION METHOD

1. Preheat the oven to 200°C (180°C fan) /
   400F / gas 6.

2. Cook the potatoes in boiling salted water
   for 12 minutes or until tender then drain
   well.

3. Meanwhile, put the milk and bay leaf in a
   small saucepan and bring to a simmer.
   Lay the haddock in a snugly-fitting dish
   and pour the hot milk over the top. Cover
   the dish with cling film and leave to stand
   for 10 minutes.

4. Heat half of the butter in a small saucepan
   and stir in the flour. Reserve 2 tablespoons
   of the haddock milk for the potatoes and
   strain the rest into the butter and flour
   mixture, stirring constantly. Cook until the
   sauce is thick and smooth.

5. Remove any skin and bones from the
   haddock then flake the flesh into the white
   sauce with the vegetables. Season to taste
   with salt and black pepper then pour the
   mixture into a baking dish.

6. Mash the potatoes with the reserved milk
   and remaining butter and spoon it on top
   of the haddock. Sprinkle with cheese then
   bake for 30 minutes or until the topping is
   golden brown.

Beef and onion free-form pie

PREPARATION TIME: 45 MINUTES I **COOKING TIME:** 1 HOUR I **SERVES:** 4

INGREDIENTS:

2 tbsp olive oil
2 red onions, sliced
3 cloves of garlic, finely chopped
450 g / 1 lb / 3 cups sirloin steak, cubed
250 g / 9 oz / 1 cup all-butter puff pastry
1 egg, beaten
salt and black pepper

PREPARATION METHOD

1. Heat the oil in a frying pan and fry the onions for 20 minutes, stirring occasionally, to soften and caramelise them. Take the pan off the heat and leave to cool, then stir in the garlic and steak and season well with salt and pepper.

2. Preheat the oven to 220°C (200°C fan) / 425F / gas 7.

3. Roll out half the pastry on a floured surface into a large circle and brush round the edge with beaten egg. Pile the filling on top. Roll out the rest of the pastry into a circle a little smaller than the base. Lay it on top, then bring up the sides of the pastry and crimp to seal. Trim away any excess and use the offcuts to decorate the top.

4. Brush the pie with egg, then bake for 40 minutes or until the pastry is cooked through and crisp underneath.

Fish and chips

PREPARATION TIME: 1 HOUR 45 MINUTES I **COOKING TIME:** 25 MINUTES I **SERVES:** 4

INGREDIENTS:

For the Fish:

200 g / 7 oz / 1 ⅓ cups plain (all-purpose)
   flour
2 tbsp olive oil
250 ml / 9 fl. oz / 1 cup pale ale
4 portions pollock fillet
lemon wedges, to garnish

rosemary sprigs, to garnish

For the chips:

4 large Maris Piper potatoes, peeled and
   cut into chips
sunflower oil for deep-frying

PREPARATION METHOD

1. Soak the potatoes in cold water for 1 hour to reduce the starch. Drain the chips and dry completely with a clean tea towel, then air-dry on a wire rack for 30 minutes.

2. Meanwhile, make the batter. Sieve the flour into a bowl then whisk in the oil and ale until smoothly combined.

3. Heat the oil in a deep fat fryer, according to the manufacturer's instructions, to a temperature of 130°C.

4. Par-cook the chips for 10 minutes so that they cook all the way through but don't brown. Drain the chips on plenty of kitchen paper to absorb the excess oil.

5. Increase the fryer temperature to 180°C. Dip the fish in the batter and fry for 6 minutes or until golden brown. Transfer the fish to a kitchen paper lined bowl and increase the fryer temperature to 190°C.

6. Return the chips to the fryer basket and cook for 4–5 minutes or until crisp and golden brown. Drain the chips of excess oil and serve with the fish immediately.

7. Garnish with lemon wedges and rosemary sprigs and sprinkle with sea salt.

Pot-roasted lamb shanks with potatoes

PREPARATION TIME: 5 MINUTES I **COOKING TIME:** 3 HOURS 15 MINUTES I **SERVES:** 4

INGREDIENTS:

4 lamb shanks
450 g / 1 lb / 2 ½ cups Jersey royal new
  potatoes
400 ml / 14 fl. oz / 1 ⅔ cups lamb stock
1 bulb of garlic, separated into cloves
a few sprigs of rosemary
a few sprigs of thyme

PREPARATION METHOD

1. Preheat the oven to 220°C (200°C fan) /
    425F / gas 7.

2. Arrange the lamb shanks in a cast iron
    casserole dish and roast in the oven,
    uncovered for 15 minutes.

3. Reduce the oven temperature to 160°C
    (140°C fan) / 325F / gas 3 and add the rest
    of the ingredients to the casserole dish.
    Cover and cook for 3 hours or until the
    meat is very tender.

4. Leave to rest for 15 minutes, then serve.

Barbecue pork belly

PREPARATION TIME: 40 MINUTES I **COOKING TIME:** 25 MINUTES I **SERVES:** 4

INGREDIENTS:

½ onion, finely grated
2 cloves garlic, crushed
2 tbsp soy sauce
1 tbsp brown sauce
1 tbsp dark brown sugar
1 tsp Worcester sauce
1 tsp Chinese five-spice powder

800 g / 1 lb 12 oz boneless pork belly,
  skin removed
pickled red cabbage and potato wedges
  to serve

PREPARATION METHOD

1. Mix the onion, garlic, soy, brown sauce, sugar, Worcester sauce, and five-spice together and massage it into the pork. Leave to marinate for 20 minutes.

2. Prepare a barbecue or preheat the grill to its highest setting.

3. Grill or barbecue the pork for 25 minutes, turning and basting occasionally, until the meat is cooked through and tender.

4. Cut into slices and serve hot or at room temperature with pickled red cabbage and potato wedges.

Gammon and pineapple with mustard

PREPARATION TIME: 5 MINUTES I **COOKING TIME:** 15 MINUTES I **SERVES:** 2

INGREDIENTS:

2 tbsp butter
2 thick gammon steaks
1 shallot, sliced
½ tsp brown mustard seeds
¼ fresh pineapple, peeled, cored, and cut
  into chunks
1 tbsp runny honey

PREPARATION METHOD

1. Heat the butter in a large frying pan and
   fry the gammon for 3 minutes on each side
   or until nicely browned. Transfer to two
   warm plates and leave to rest covered
   with foil.

2. Add the shallots and mustard seeds to the
   pan and stir-fry for 2 minutes. Add the
   pineapple and stir-fry for 3 minutes, then
   drizzle with honey.

3. Cook for 2 more minutes or until reduced
   to a sticky glaze, then spoon the pineapple
   and pan juices over the gammon steaks and
   serve immediately.

Salmon pie

PREPARATION TIME: 15 MINUTES I **COOKING TIME:** 40 MINUTES I **SERVES:** 4

INGREDIENTS:

450 g / 1 lb / 2 cups all-butter puff pastry
450 g / 1 lb / 3 cups skinless boneless
  salmon fillet, cubed
300 ml / 10 ½ fl. oz / 1 ¼ cups double
  (heavy) cream
1 tbsp Dijon mustard
2 egg yolks, beaten

2 tbsp dill, chopped
1 egg, beaten
salt and black pepper

PREPARATION METHOD

1. Preheat the oven to 200°C (180°C fan) /
   400F / gas 6.

2. Roll out half the pastry on a floured surface
   and use it to line a gratin dish. Arrange the
   salmon on top in an even layer.

3. Mix the cream with the mustard, egg yolks,
   and dill and season with salt and white
   pepper, then pour it over the salmon.

4. Roll out the rest of the pastry and lay
   it on top. Trim away any excess and
   crimp round the edge, then brush it with
   beaten egg. Use any offcuts to decorate
   the top, attaching them with a little more
   beaten egg.

5. Bake the pie for 40 minutes or until the
   pastry is cooked through underneath and
   golden brown on top.

Sea bass

PREPARATION TIME: 5 MINUTES | **COOKING TIME:** 5 MINUTES | **SERVES:** 4

INGREDIENTS:

4 sea bass fillets, halved
12 artichoke hearts, defrosted if frozen
4 tbsp olive oil
2 tbsp basil leaves, shredded
½ lemon
a pinch of cayenne pepper

PREPARATION METHOD

1. Steam the sea bass and artichoke hearts for 5 minutes or until the artichokes are tender and the sea bass has just turned opaque in the centre.

2. Meanwhile, put the oil and basil in a small saucepan and warm through over a gentle heat to infuse. Add a squeeze of lemon and a sprinkle of cayenne pepper, then drizzle it over the sea bass and artichokes and serve immediately.

Creamy chicken and leek pie

PREPARATION TIME: 30 MINUTES I **COOKING TIME:** 45 MINUTES I **SERVES:** 4

INGREDIENTS:

2 tbsp butter
2 leeks, sliced
1 tbsp plain (all-purpose) flour
250 ml / 9 fl. oz / 1 cups milk
3 cooked chicken breasts, cubed
150 ml / 5 ½ fl. oz / ⅔ cup crème fraiche
½ tsp freshly grated nutmeg

2 tbsp French tarragon, finely chopped
450 g / 1 lb / 2 cups all-butter puff pastry
1 egg, beaten
salt and black pepper

PREPARATION METHOD

1. Heat the butter in a saucepan and fry the leeks for 10 minutes without colouring. Sprinkle in the flour and stir well, then stir in the milk and bubble until it thickens. Add the chicken and crème fraiche and heat through, then season to taste with salt and white pepper. Stir in the nutmeg and tarragon then leave to cool completely.

2. Preheat the oven to 200°C (180°C fan) / 400F / gas 6.

3. Roll out half the pastry on a lightly floured surface and use it to line a pie dish. Spoon in the filling and level the top, then brush round the rim with water. Roll out the rest of the pastry and lay it over the top, then trim away any excess and make a hole in the centre for the steam to escape.

4. Brush the top of the pie with beaten egg then bake for 45 minutes or until the pastry is cooked through underneath and golden brown on top.

Cakes

Marmalade Swiss roll

PREPARATION TIME: 15 MINUTES I **COOKING TIME:** 15–20 MINUTES I **SERVES:** 6

INGREDIENTS:

100 g / 3 ½ oz / ⅔ cup self-raising flour
1 tsp baking powder
100 g / 3 ½ oz / ½ cup caster
  (superfine) sugar
100 g / 3 ½ oz / ½ cup butter
2 large eggs

1 tsp vanilla extract
350 g / 12 oz / 1 cup marmalade

PREPARATION METHOD

1. Preheat the oven to 180°C (160°C fan) /
    350F / gas 4 and grease and line a Swiss
    roll tin.

2. Put all of the ingredients, except the
    marmalade, in a large mixing bowl and
    whisk together with an electric whisk for
    4 minutes or until pale and well whipped.
    Spoon the mixture into the tin and spread
    into an even layer with a palette knife.

3. Bake for 15–20 minutes or until the cake is
    springy to the touch.

4. Turn the cake out onto a sheet of
    greaseproof paper and peel off the lining
    paper. Spread the cake with marmalade
    then roll it up tightly and leave to cool
    before slicing.

Lemon and poppy seed cake

PREPARATION TIME: 15 MINUTES **I COOKING TIME:** 55 MINUTES **I SERVES:** 8

INGREDIENTS:

225 g / 8 oz / 1 ½ cups self-raising flour
100 g / 3 ½ oz / ½ cup butter, cubed
100 g / 3 ½ oz / ½ cup caster (superfine)
  sugar
3 tbsp poppy seeds
1 large egg

75 ml / 2 ½ fl. oz / $^1/_3$ cup whole milk
1 lemon, juiced and zest finely grated

PREPARATION METHOD

1. Preheat the oven to 180°C (160°C fan) /
    355F / gas 4 and line a 23 cm (9 in) round
    cake tin with non-stick baking paper.

2. Sieve the flour into a mixing bowl and
    rub in the butter until it resembles fine
    breadcrumbs, then stir in the sugar and
    poppy seeds.

3. Lightly beat the egg with the milk, lemon
    juice, and lemon zest and stir it into the dry
    ingredients until just combined.

4. Scrape the mixture into the tin and bake
    for 55 minutes or until a skewer inserted
    comes out clean. Transfer the cake to a wire
    rack and leave to cool completely.

Sultana scones with cream and jam

PREPARATION TIME: 25 MINUTES I **COOKING TIME:** 15 MINUTES I **MAKES:** 12

INGREDIENTS:

225 g / 8 oz / 1 ½ cups self-raising flour
55 g / 2 oz / ¼ cup butter, plus extra for
  spreading
75 g / 2 ½ oz / ⅓ cup sultanas
150 ml / 5 fl. oz / ⅔ cup whole milk
1 egg, beaten

200 g / 7 oz / ¾ cup double (heavy) cream
200 g / 7 oz / ¾ cup strawberry jam (jelly)

PREPARATION METHOD

1. Preheat the oven to 220°C (200°C fan) /
   425F / gas 7 and oil a large baking sheet.

2. Sieve the flour into a bowl and rub in the
   butter until the mixture resembles fine
   breadcrumbs. Stir in the sultanas with
   enough milk to bring the mixture together
   into a soft dough.

3. Flatten the dough with your hands on a
   floured work surface until 2.5 cm (1 in)
   thick. Use a pastry cutter to cut out 12
   circles and transfer them to the prepared
   baking sheet.

4. Brush the scones with beaten egg then
   bake for 15 minutes or until golden brown
   and cooked through. Transfer the scones to
   a wire rack to cool completely.

5. Whip the cream until it just holds its shape.
   When the scones have cooled, spread them
   with cream and top with a spoonful of jam.

Mini Victoria sponges

PREPARATION TIME: 45 MINUTES I **COOKING TIME:** 30 MINUTES I **MAKES:** 8

INGREDIENTS:

200 g / 7 oz / 1 ⅓ cups self-raising flour
200 g / 7 oz / ¾ cup caster (superfine) sugar
200 g / 7 oz / ¾ cup butter
4 large eggs
1 tsp baking powder
1 tsp vanilla extract

To decorate:
100 g / 3 ½ oz / ½ cup butter, softened
200 g / 7 oz / 2 cups icing (confectioners')
   sugar, plus extra for dusting
300 g / 10 ½ oz / 1 ¼ cups strawberry
   jam (jelly)

PREPARATION METHOD

1. Preheat the oven to 180°C (160°C fan)
    / 350F / gas 4 and grease and line a
    20 cm x 30 cm (8 in x 12 in) cake tin
    with greaseproof paper.

2. Put all of the cake ingredients in a large
    mixing bowl and whisk with an electric
    whisk for 4 minutes or until pale and
    well whipped. Scrape the mixture into
    the prepared tin and level the top with
    a spatula.

3. Bake for 30 minutes or until a skewer
    inserted comes out clean. Transfer the cake
    to a wire rack and leave to cool completely.

4. To make the buttercream, whisk the butter
    with an electric whisk then gradually add
    the icing sugar. Whisk until smooth and
    well whipped. If the mixture is too stiff, add
    a tablespoon of warm water.

5. Use a round cookie cutter to cut out 16
    circles of cake. Spread 8 of the circles with
    jam and buttercream, then top with the rest
    of the cake circles and dust liberally with
    icing sugar.

Desserts

Apple crumble

PREPARATION TIME: 15 MINUTES | **COOKING TIME:** 45 MINUTES | **SERVES:** 6

INGREDIENTS:

2 large bramley apples, peeled, cored
and chopped
2 eating apples, peeled, cored and chopped
4 tbsp caster (superfine) sugar
75 g / 2 ½ oz / ⅓ cup butter
50 g / 1 ¾ oz / ⅓ cup plain (all-purpose)
flour

25 g / 1 oz / ¼ cup ground almonds
40 g / 1 ½ oz / ¼ cup light brown sugar

PREPARATION METHOD

1. Preheat the oven to 180°C (160°C fan) /
350F / gas 4.

2. Mix the apples with the sugar and arrange
in the bottom of a baking dish.

3. Rub the butter into the flour and stir in the
ground almonds and brown sugar. Squeeze
a handful of the mixture into a clump and
then crumble it over the fruit. Use up the
rest of the topping in the same way, then
shake the dish to level the top.

4. Bake the crumble for 45 minutes or until
the topping is golden brown and the fruit
is bubbling.

Cherry and almond tart

PREPARATION TIME: 1 HOUR I **COOKING TIME:** 40 MINUTES I **SERVES:** 8

INGREDIENTS:

110 g / 4 oz / ½ cup butter, cubed and chilled
225 g / 8 oz / 1 ½ cups plain (all-purpose)
   flour
150 g / 5 ½ oz / 1 cup black cherries, stoned
icing (confectioners') sugar for dusting

For the frangipane:
55 g / 2 oz / ½ cup ground almonds
55 g / 2 oz / ¼ cup caster (superfine) sugar
55 g / 2 oz / ¼ cup butter, softened
1 large egg
1 tsp almond essence

PREPARATION METHOD

1. Rub the butter into the flour then add just enough cold water to bind the mixture together into a pliable dough. Roll out the pastry on a floured surface and use it to line a 23 cm (9 in) round tart case. Leave the pastry to chill the fridge for 30 minutes.

2. Preheat the oven to 200°C (180°C fan) / 400F / gas 6.

3. Line the pastry case with cling film and fill it with baking beans, then bake for 15 minutes.

4. To make the frangipane, combine the ground almonds, sugar, butter, egg and almond essence in a bowl and whisk together for 2 minutes or until smooth. Fold in the cherries.

5. When the pastry case is ready, remove the cling film and baking beans and fill the case with frangipane. Bake for 25 minutes or until set in the centre, then dust with icing sugar.

Speedy summer fruit trifle

PREPARATION TIME: 30 MINUTES I **SERVES:** 8

INGREDIENTS:

300 g / 10 ½ oz lemon madeira cake, sliced
4 tbsp limoncello
50 g / 1 ¾ oz / ½ cup icing (confectioners')
   sugar
225 g / 8 oz / 1 cup Greek yoghurt
225 g / 8 oz / 1 cup mascarpone

200 g / 7 oz / 1 ⅓ cups raspberries
200 g / 7 oz / 1 ⅓ cups blueberries

PREPARATION METHOD

1. Lay half of the cake slices in a trifle bowl
    and sprinkle with half of the limoncello.

2. Fold the icing sugar into the yoghurt and
    mascarpone, then spoon half of it over
    the cake.

3. Top with half of the berries, then cover with
    the rest of the cake and limoncello. Spoon
    the rest of the yoghurt mixture on top and
    scatter over the rest of the berries.

4. Chill in the fridge for 20 minutes for the
    flavours to infuse before serving.

Mixed berry mess

PREPARATION TIME: 10 MINUTES I **SERVES:** 4

INGREDIENTS:

400 ml / 14 fl. oz / 1 ⅔ cups double (heavy)
   cream
1 tsp vanilla extract
2 tbsp icing (confectioners') sugar
4 meringue nests
150 g / 5 ½ oz / 1 cup mixed summer berries

PREPARATION METHOD

1. Whip the cream with the vanilla and
    icing sugar until it just holds its shape,
    then spoon two quenelles onto each of
    four plates.

2. Break the meringue nests into chunks and
    scatter them over the top with the berries.
    Serve immediately.

Individual bread and butter puddings

PREPARATION TIME: 20 MINUTES I **COOKING TIME:** 1 HOUR I **MAKES:** 4

INGREDIENTS:

4 thick slices white bread
3 tbsp butter, softened
4 tbsp sultanas
250 ml / 9 fl. oz / 1 cup milk
200 ml / 7 fl. oz / ¾ cup double (heavy)
  cream

4 large egg yolks
75 g / 2 ½ oz / ⅓ cup caster (superfine)
  sugar
1 lemon, zest finely grated
nutmeg to grate

PREPARATION METHOD

1. Spread the bread with butter and cut each piece into four triangles. Butter four small baking dishes and layer up the bread inside with the sultanas.

2. Whisk the milk, cream, eggs, sugar, and lemon zest together and divide it between the dishes, then leave to soak for 10 minutes.

3. Preheat the oven to 150°C (130°C fan) / 300F / gas 2.

4. Bake the puddings for 1 hour or until the custard is just set with a slight wobble. Grate over a little nutmeg and serve hot or cold.

Rhubarb and ginger crumble

PREPARATION TIME: 15 MINUTES I **COOKING TIME:** 45 MINUTES I **SERVES:** 4

INGREDIENTS:

450 g / 1 lb / 2 ½ cups rhubarb, cut into
 short lengths
2 pieces of stem ginger, finely chopped
4 tbsp caster (superfine) sugar
75 g / 2 ½ oz / ⅓ cup butter
50 g / 1 ¾ oz / ⅓ cup plain (all-purpose)
 flour

1 tsp ground ginger
25 g / 1 oz / ¼ cup ground almonds
40 g / 1 ½ oz / ¼ cup light brown sugar

PREPARATION METHOD

1. Preheat the oven to 180°C (160°C fan) /
   350F / gas 4.

2. Mix the rhubarb with the stem ginger and
   caster sugar and arrange in the bottom of a
   baking dish.

3. Rub the butter into the flour and stir in
   the ground ginger, ground almonds, and
   brown sugar. Squeeze a handful of the
   mixture into a clump and then crumble
   it over the fruit. Use up the rest of the
   topping in the same way, then shake the
   dish to level the top.

4. Bake the crumble for 45 minutes or until
   the topping is golden brown and the fruit is
   bubbling.

Rice pudding with strawberries

PREPARATION TIME: 15 MINUTES I **COOKING TIME:** 1 HOUR 30 MINUTES I **SERVES:** 6

INGREDIENTS:

110 g / 4 oz / ½ cup short-grain rice
75 g / 2 ½ oz / ⅓ cup caster (superfine)
   sugar
1.2 litres / 2 pints / 4 ½ cups whole milk
250 g / 9 oz / 1 ⅔ cups strawberries, halved
icing (confectioners') sugar for dusting
lavender leaves to garnish

PREPARATION METHOD

1. Preheat the oven to 140°C (120°C fan) /
   275F / gas 1.

2. Stir the rice and sugar into the milk in a
   baking dish, then cover and bake for
   1 hour 30 minutes. Leave to cool
   completely.

3. Discard the skin on top of the pudding and
   use a ring mould to portion the rice onto
   6 plates.

4. Top with the strawberries then dust with
   icing sugar and garnish with lavender
   leaves.

Strawberry jelly

PREPARATION TIME: 15 MINUTES I **COOKING TIME:** 5 MINS
CHILLING TIME: 2–3 HOURS I **SERVES:** 4

INGREDIENTS:

4 gelatine leaves
600 ml / 1 pint / 2 ½ cups strawberry juice drink

PREPARATION METHOD

1. Soak the gelatine in a small bowl of cold water for 10 minutes.

2. Heat 200 ml of the juice in a small saucepan until it starts to simmer, then turn off the heat.

3. Squeeze any excess liquid out of the softened gelatine then whisk it into the hot juice to dissolve. Stir the hot gelatine mixture into the rest of the cold juice then pour it into a jelly mould.

4. Transfer the mould carefully to the fridge and leave to chill and set for 2–3 hours.

5. When you are ready to serve, dip the outside of the mould briefly in a bowl of hot water, making sure no water gets into the jelly. Give it a shake to loosen, then turn the jelly out onto a plate.

Apple pie

PREPARATION TIME: 20 MINUTES I **COOKING TIME:** 40 MINUTES I **SERVES:** 6

INGREDIENTS:

2 bramley apples, peeled, cored, and thinly
  sliced
1 tsp ground cinnamon
1 tsp cornflour (cornstarch)
3 tbsp caster (superfine) sugar

For the pastry:
200 g / 7 oz / 1 cup butter, cubed and chilled
400 g / 14 oz / 2 ⅔ cups plain (all-purpose)
  flour
2 tbsp milk
2 tbsp demerara sugar

PREPARATION METHOD

1. Preheat the oven to 200°C (180°C fan) /
   400F / gas 6.

2. To make the pastry, rub the butter into the
   flour then add just enough cold water to
   form a pliable dough. Roll out half of the
   pastry on a floured surface and use it to
   line a pie dish.

3. Toss the apples with the cinnamon,
   cornflour, and sugar, then pack the mixture
   into the pastry case.

4. Roll out the rest of the pastry and lay it
   over the top. Trim away any excess and
   crimp to seal. Make a hole in the centre for
   the steam to escape.

5. Brush the top of the pie with milk and
   sprinkle with sugar, then bake for 40
   minutes or until the pastry is cooked
   through underneath and golden brown
   on top.

Chilled white chocolate cake

PREPARATION TIME: 20 MINUTES I **COOKING TIME:** 5 MINUTES
CHILLING TIME: 4 HOURS I **MAKES:** 6

INGREDIENTS:

300 g / 10 ½ oz white chocolate, chopped
100 g / 3 ½ oz / ½ cup butter
100 g / 3 ½ oz / ½ cup caster (superfine) sugar
3 medium egg yolks
250 g / 9 oz coconut biscuits

300 ml / 10 ½ fl. oz / 1 ¼ cups double (heavy) cream, whipped
150 g / 5 ½ oz / 1 cup strawberries, halved

PREPARATION METHOD

1. Melt the chocolate and butter together over a low heat in a saucepan, then remove from the heat.

2. Whisk the sugar and egg yolks together until pale and thick, then fold in the chocolate mixture until smoothly combined.

3. Reserve two biscuits for decoration, then put the rest in a sandwich bag and crush with a rolling pin. Fold the crushed biscuits into the chocolate mixture.

4. Pack 6 ring moulds with the mixture and level the tops. Transfer the tin to the fridge and leave to set for at least 4 hours.

5. Unmould the cakes and top with whipped cream, strawberries, and the reserved biscuits crumbled over the top.

Steamed chocolate puddings

PREPARATION TIME: 30 MINUTES I **COOKING TIME:** 1 HOUR I **MAKES:** 8

INGREDIENTS:

200 g / 7 oz / 1 1/3 cups self-raising flour
200 g / 7 oz / 3/4 cup dark brown sugar
200 g / 7 oz / 3/4 cup butter
4 large eggs
1 tsp baking powder
3 tbsp unsweetened cocoa powder

For the sauce:
200 ml / 7 fl. oz / 3/4 cup double (heavy) cream
200 g / 7 oz dark chocolate, minimum 60% cocoa solids, chopped

PREPARATION METHOD

1. Butter eight individual pudding basins and put a steamer on to heat.

2. Put all of the cake ingredients in a large mixing bowl and whisk with an electric whisk for 4 minutes.

3. Divide the mixture between the pudding basins then transfer them to the steamer and steam for 1 hour.

4. Towards the end of the cooking time, heat the cream until it starts to simmer, then pour it over the chopped chocolate and stir until smooth.

5. Carefully unmould the puddings onto warm plates and pour over the sauce.

Index